Other books by Exley:
An Illustrated Country Notebook
An Illustrated Gardener's Notebook
Flowers – A Celebration
Garden Lover's Quotations

In the same series:
Address Books:
The Illustrated Cats Address Book
The Illustrated Flower Arranging Address Book
The Illustrated Gardening Address Book
The Illustrated Golf Address Book
The Illustrated Horse Address Book
The Illustrated Motoring Address Book
The Illustrated Sailing Address Book
The Illustrated Tea Address Book
Day Book:
The Garden Lover's Book of Days

Other Illustrated Stationery Books:
Guest Book
Household Record Book

Front cover: *Wild Flowers in a Vase* – Eugene-Henri Cauchois
(Fine Art Photographic Library)
Frontispiece: *A Vase of Chrysanthemums* – Eugene Petit
(Fine Art Photographic Library)

First published in the USA in 1992 by Exley Giftbooks
Published in Great Britain in 1989 by Exley Publications Ltd
Reprinted 1990
Third printing 1992
Fourth printing 1993

Copyright © Exley Publications Ltd, 1989
Selection copyright © Helen Exley 1992
ISBN 1-85015-160-1

Picture research: Kate Duffy, Karen Gunnell, Diana Briscoe.
Printed and bound in Hungary.

Exley Publications, 16 Chalk Hill, Watford, Herts WD1 4BN, United Kingdom.
Exley Giftbooks, 359 East Main Street, Suite 3D, Mount Kisco, NY 10549, USA.

The FLOWER LOVERS

BIRTHDAY BOOK

EXLEY

Notes

‎𝒩OTES

When at last I took the time to look into the heart of a flower, it opened up a whole new world... as if a window had been opened to let in the sun.

PRINCESS GRACE OF MONACO

NOTES

NOTES

_____
_____
_____
_____
_____
_____
_____
_____
_____
_____
_____
_____
_____
_____
_____
_____
_____
_____

Wildflowers are perhaps the most enchanting
of all for me. I love their delicacy,
their disarming innocence, and their defiance
of life itself.

PRINCESS GRACE OF MONACO

How many daisies can you count on your lawn?
When you can count twelve daisies,
spring has come.

ELEANOR FARJEON

JANUARY

1

2

3

4

5

6

7

STILL LIFE
*JOSHUA
ANDERSON
HAGUE*
*Phillips Fine Art
Auctioneers*

$\mathcal{J}$ANUARY

8

9

10

11

12

13

14

JANUARY

15

16

17

18

19

20

21

A VASE OF
FLOWERS, 1910
*MAXIME
MAUFRA*
*Fine Art Photographic
Library*

No one forgets the flowers of childhood. PAM BROWN

JANUARY

_____

22

_____

23

_____

24

_____

25

_____

26

_____

27

_____

28

FLOWERS
[PASTEL]
ODILON REDON
Bridgeman-Giraudon:
Brame-Lorenceau,
the Old Collection

Earth laughs in flowers. RALPH WALDO EMERSON

_____

JANUARY/FEBRUARY

29

30

31

1

2

3

4

*What a desolate place would be a world
without flowers! It would be a face without
a smile, a feast without a welcome.*

CLARA L. BALFOUR

*Where would we be if humanity had never known
flowers? If they didn't exist or had always
been hidden from our sight... would our
character, our morals, our aptitude for
beauty, our happiness be the same?*

MAURICE MAETERLINCK

There is no such thing as an ordinary flower.

CHARLOTTE GRAY

ℱEBRUARY

5

6

7

8

9

10

11

STILL LIFE WITH
ROSES IN A VASE
*SAMUEL JOHN
PEPLOE*
*Fine Art Photographic
Library*

Nobody sees a flower - really - it is so
small - we haven't time - and to see takes
time like to have a friend takes time.

GEORGIA O'KEEFFE

FEBRUARY

12

_____

13

_____

14

_____

15

_____

16

_____

17

_____

18

FEBRUARY

19

20

21

22

23

24

25

WHITE
NARCISSUS,
HYACINTHS AND
TULIPS
HENRI FANTIN-LATOUR
*Bridgeman Art Library:
Private Collection*

A house with daffodils in it is a house lit up... A. A. MILNE

26

27

28/29

1

2

3

STUDY OF
FLOWERS IN A
VASE
*JOHN
CONSTABLE*
*Scala: London, Victoria
and Albert Museum*

4

$\mathcal{M}$ARCH

5

6

7

8

9

10

11

One flower is worth an hour's wonder.   PAM BROWN

MARCH

12

13

14

15

16

17

18

Love of flowers has opened many doors for me.
In the last twelve years I have made many
friends throughout the world who fascinate me
because of their love and outstanding
knowledge of flowers.

PRINCESS GRACE OF MONACO

$\mathcal{M}$ARCH

19

_____

20

_____

21

_____

22

_____

23

_____

24

_____

25

STILL LIFE
ARTHUR
CHAPLIN
Bridgeman Art Library:
Hamm-Rhynern, Josef
Mensing Gallery

_____

26

27

28

29

30

31

1

MIXED FLOWERS
IN A JUG
ODILON REDON
Bridgeman Art Library

The only hunger of our souls is for dreams and flowers. PAUL-JEAN TOULET

$\mathscr{A}$PRIL

2

3

4

5

6

7

8

Each flower is a soul that blossoms out of nature. GERARD DE NERVAL

APRIL

9

10

11

12

13

14

15

Never yet was a springtime when the buds forgot to blow. MARGARET SANGSTER

APRIL

16

17

18

19

20

21

22

*There is no monotony in flowers, they are
ever unfolding new charms, developing new
forms and revealing new features of interest
and beauty to those who love them.*

JOHN WRIGHT, c.1890

APRIL

23

24

25

26

27

28

29

SPRING FLOWERS
IN A VASE
ON A TABLE
EMILY PATRICK
Bridgeman Art Library:
Private Collection

*Ah, everything has changed since I was a
girl, except my flowers; that is why I have
them so near me, for they are my oldest
friends, so I give them the place of honour.*

from JOURNAL OF HORTICULTURE, 1863

*Were the flowers of the world to be taken
away, they would leave a blank in creation.
Imagination cannot suggest a substitute for
them. Whether they flourish in the garden,
or bloom in the greenhouse; whether they are
scattered in our pathway, sprinkled on the
verdant banks, or widely strewn over the
hills and vales, they never fail to please;
they fill the air with their sweetness; and
delight the eye with their beauty.*

ANON, c.1870

APRIL/MAY

30

1

2

3

4

5

6

$\mathcal{M}$AY

7

8

9

10

11

12

13

*M*AY

14

15

16

17

18

19

20

To analyze the charms of flowers is like dissecting music. H. T. TUCKERMAN

MAY

21

22

23

24

25

26

27

Many eyes go through the meadow, but few see the flowers... RALPH WALDO EMERSON

$\mathcal{M}$AY / $\mathcal{J}$UNE

28

29

30

31

1

2

STILL LIFE OF
CARNATIONS AND
TULIPS

*JEAN BAPTISTE
MONNOYER*
*Bridgeman Art Library:
London, Johnny van
Haeften*

3

JUNE

4

5

6

7

8

9

10

JUNE

11

12

13

14

15

16

17

JUNE

18

_____

19

_____

20

_____

21

_____

22

_____

23

_____

24

DAHLIAS, ROSES
AND GLADIOLI
*HENRI FANTIN-
LATOUR*
*Bridgeman-Giraudon:
Brame et Lorenceau,
the Old Collection*

There is no such thing as an ordinary flower. PAM BROWN

JUNE/JULY

25

26

27

28

29

30

1

July

2

3

4

5

6

7

8

JULY

9

10

11

12

13

14

15

... the earth, gentle and indulgent,
ever subservient
to the wants of man,
spreads his walks with flowers,
and his table with plenty;
returns with interest, every good
committed to her care.

PLINY THE ELDER

JULY

16
_____

17
_____

18
_____

19
_____

20
_____

21
_____

22

JULY

23

24

25

26

27

28

29

Art is the unceasing effort to compete with
the beauty of flowers - and never succeeding.

MARC CHAGALL

JULY/AUGUST

30

31

1

2

3

4

5

AUGUST

6

7

8

9

10

11

12

ROSE "FANTIN
LATOUR" & BASKET
OF STRAWBERRIES
ON A SHELF
PAMELA KAY
Bridgeman Art Library:
Chris Beetles Ltd

*Arranging a bowl of flowers in the morning
can give a sense of quiet in a crowded day -
like writing a poem, or saying a prayer.*

ANNE MORROW LINDBERGH

*Flowers reflect the human search for meaning.
Does not each of us, no matter how our life
has gone, ache to have a life as beautiful
and true to itself as that of a flower?*

PHILIP MOFFITT

*We have no words so complex, so delicate, so
simple or so strong as flowers. Therefore we
let them speak for us.*

PAM BROWN

AUGUST

13

14

15

16

17

18

19

AUGUST

20

21

22

23

24

25

26

AUGUST/SEPTEMBER

27

28

29

30

31

1

2

To create a little flower is the labour of ages. WILLIAM BLAKE

SEPTEMBER

3

4

5

6

7

8

9

ONE-EARED VASE
WITH
HOLLYHOCKS
*VINCENT VAN
GOGH*
*Bridgeman Art Library:
Zurich, Kunsthaus*

SEPTEMBER

10

11

12

13

14

15

16

What other planet smells of roses? PAM BROWN

SEPTEMBER

17

18

19

20

21

22

23

So much of the beauty of a flower is in its very perishableness. DENISE LEVERTOV

$\mathcal{S}$EPTEMBER

24

25

26

27

28

29

30

WHITE PEONIES
WITH ROSES AND
NARCISSUS
*HENRI FANTIN-
LATOUR*
*Bridgeman Art Library:
Private Collection*

OCTOBER

1

2

3

4

5

6

7

There are strange evenings when the flowers have a soul. ALBERT SAMAIN

OCTOBER

8

9

10

11

12

13

14

FLOWERS
*EUGENE
DELACROIX*
*Bridgeman Art Library:
Lille, Musée des
Beaux Arts*

*Some flowers spoke with strong and powerful
voices, which proclaimed in accents trumpet-
tongued, "I am beautiful, and I rule."
Others murmured in tones scarcely audible,
but exquisitely soft and sweet, "I am little,
and I am beloved."*

GEORGE SAND

OCTOBER

15

16

17

18

19

20

21

FLOWERS IN A
TURQUOISE VASE
ODILON REDON
Giraudon: Berne,
Musée Hahnlose

Flowers... are the poor man's poetry. ANNE PRATT

OCTOBER

22

23

24

25

26

27

28

OCTOBER/NOVEMBER

29

30

31

1

2

3

4

To be overpowered by the fragrance of flowers
is a delectable form of defeat.

BEVERLY NICHOLS

NOVEMBER

5

6

7

8

9

10

11

STILL LIFE OF
ROSES IN A VASE
*SAMUEL JOHN
PEPLOE*
*Fine Art Photographic
Library*

NOVEMBER

12

13

14

15

16

17

18

Hast thou loved the wood-rose and left it on its stalk?

RALPH WALDO EMERSON (1803-1882)

NOVEMBER

19

20

21

22

23

24

25

PURPLE POPPIES
CLAUDE MONET
Bridgeman Art Library:
Rotterdam, Museum
Boymans van Beuningen

NOVEMBER/ DECEMBER

26

27

28

29

30

1

2

STILL LIFE WITH
FLOWERS
*CHARLES
GINNER*
*Bridgeman Art Library:
York Art Gallery*

How cool, how delicate, how intricate a flower.
They teach us gentleness of touch.
They teach us how to see. They waken the heart.

PAM BROWN

DECEMBER

3

4

5

6

7

8

9

STILL LIFE OF
PINK ROSES IN A
GLASS VASE
*FRANS
MORTELMANS*
*Fine Art Photographic
Library*

DECEMBER

10

11

12

13

14

15

16

DECEMBER

17

18

19

20

21

22

23

STILL LIFE
SIMON VERELST
Bridgeman Art Library;
London, Alan Jacobs
Gallery

Where would we be if humanity had never known flowers? MAURICE MAETERLINCK

DECEMBER

24

25

26

27

28

29

30

Thanks to the human heart by which we live,
Thanks to its tenderness, its joys and fears,
To me the meanest flower that blows can give
Thoughts that do often lie too deep for
tears.

WILLIAM WORDSWORTH

DECEMBER / JANUARY

31

1

2

3

4

5

6